trees

plants need trees

people need trees

"Trees give us so many things that we need. But not only people need trees for food and shelter. That's why we must save trees and plant trees."

Grusilda xxx

WWW.THELITERACYTOWER.COM

We should always try to save trees.

Trees are home for many animals like insects, birds and reptiles.

Insects live in trees.

Birds live in trees.

Reptiles live in trees.

We should always try to plant new trees.

Trees give animals many things they need, like food and shelter.

Trees give animals food.

Trees give birds a home.

Trees give animals shelter.

Trees help to keep our air clean.

Trees can grow fruit for us to eat.

An orange is a fruit that grows on a tree.

An apple is a fruit that grows on a tree.

A peach is a fruit that grows on a tree.

Trees give us shade on a sunny day.

Trees give us wood for homes.

Many plants and animals use old trees that fall down and rot.

Trees that fall down can give homes to tiny plants and other living things.

Trees that fall down and rot can give food to tiny animals and other living things.

What can we do when trees are cut down?

1. We can plant new trees.
2. We can look after all trees.

Two children plant new trees.

A boy puts water on a tree.

We can build houses without cutting more trees down.

Most of all,
we should learn
more about trees.
Trees can be
our **biggest** friends.